Tundra

PETER BENOIT

Children's Press®
An Imprint of Scholastic Inc.
New York   Toronto   London   Auckland   Sydney
Mexico City   New Delhi   Hong Kong
Danbury, Connecticut

Content Consultant
Lee W. Cooper, PhD
Chesapeake Biological Lab, University of Maryland
Solomons, Maryland

Library of Congress Cataloging-in-Publication Data

Benoit, Peter, 1955–
  Tundra/Peter Benoit.
      p. cm.—(A true book)
  Includes bibliographical references and index.
  ISBN-13: 978-0-531-20553-2 (lib. bdg.)   978-0-531-28102-4 (pbk.)
  ISBN-10: 0-531-20553-3 (lib. bdg.)   0-531-28102-7 (pbk.)
  1. Tundra ecology—Juvenile literature. 2. Tundras—Juvenile literature. I. Title.
  QH541.5.T8B46 2011
  577.5'86—dc22   2010045934

All rights reserved. Published in 2011 by Children's Press, an imprint of Scholastic Inc.
Printed in China. 62
SCHOLASTIC, CHILDREN'S PRESS, A TRUE BOOK and associated logos are trademarks and/or registered trademarks of Scholastic Inc.

1 2 3 4 5 6 7 8 9 10 R 18 17 16 15 14 13 12 11

Find the Truth!

Everything you are about to read is true *except* for one of the sentences on this page.

Which one is **TRUE**?

T or F Tundra is too cold for insects.

T or F Permafrost contains methane.

Find the answers in this book.

3

Contents

THE BIG TRUTH!

Land of the Giants

Polar bear fur is clear, not white. It looks white because it reflects light. ➡

Skeleton of a
mammoth

A backpacker overlooks warped trees in the White Mountains of New Hampshire.

CHAPTER 1

Up the Mountain

A group of hikers set off on a trail in New Hampshire's White Mountains. At the bottom, it was 80 degrees Fahrenheit (27 degrees Celsius). The air grew cooler as they hiked up the trail. As they climbed, the balsam fir and black spruce trees got shorter. Soon, the trees around them started to look different. They were twisted into strange shapes with branches growing on only one side.

 Both the trees and the air get thinner at higher altitudes.

Into the Tundra

Farther up the trail, the trees became woody shrubs growing on rocks. Then there were no trees at all. The hikers climbed through a world of rocks covered in moss and lichen (LYE-ken). Near the mountain's top, the temperature was 35°F (2°C). Winds howled at 50 miles per hour (80 kilometers per hour). Though it was July 4, snow covered the ground. The hikers had entered the heart of the tundra.

A man leans into fierce winds at the observation deck on Mount Washington in the White Mountains.

The region between forested areas and the tundra is called the tree line.

Alpine tundra is found above the tree line on tall, cold mountains.

Tundra Basics

In a tundra **ecosystem**, temperatures may average above 32°F (0°C) for a month or two. They never average more than 50°F (10°C). Cold temperatures and the short summers **stunt** plant growth. Plants hug the ground. Moss, lichens, and grasses are found on the tundra. So are shrubs and **sedges**. Some tundra ecosystems feature permanent ice and snow. In others, cool summers break up a long winter.

CHAPTER 2

Tundra Types

There are three types of tundra: Arctic, Antarctic, and alpine. Arctic tundra is found at far northern **latitudes** in places such as Russia, Alaska, Canada, Greenland, and Scandinavia. Antarctic tundra is only found in Antarctica. Alpine tundra can be seen on mountaintops all around the world.

This map shows where tundra is found.

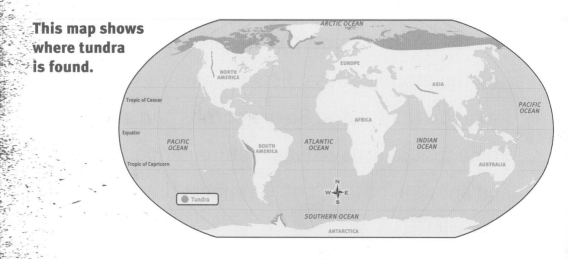

Tundra means "treeless plain" in the language of the Sami, a people living in northern Scandinavia.

Scandinavia is a region of Europe that includes the countries of Denmark, Norway, and Sweden.

One major feature of the tundra is **permafrost**— soil below the surface that is frozen most or all of the year. Few trees can grow in permafrost. The willow species survives by sending out roots along the top of the frozen ground.

Permafrost Hill

Permafrost is a powerful force that shapes the land. Sometimes wet soil becomes trapped between two permafrost layers. The heavy permafrost squeezes the moisture from the soil. The moisture then freezes and takes up more space. As the ice expands, it pushes the permafrost upward. This forms a cone-shaped hill called a pingo. A pingo can rise to 300 feet (90 meters).

One-fourth of all the pingos in the world lie in Canada's Northwest Territories.

Thawing permafrost forms lakes because water cannot drain through the frozen ground.

During the summer, lakes form in the tundra.

Arctic Summer

Arctic summer temperatures of 50°F (10°C) or higher melt the top permafrost layer. This thawed soil is called the **active layer**. Water pools and forms marshes, lakes, and streams. The summer sun shines in the sky 20 or more hours per day. Plants take advantage of the water and sun. The growing season lasts 50 to 60 days. About 1,700 species on Earth can grow in tundra.

In winter, the fur of the Arctic fox turns from gray or grayish brown to white to help it blend into its surroundings.

The Living Tundra

Animal activity comes alive in summer. Millions of geese, ducks, and other waterbirds fly from the south to find mates and lay eggs. **Predators** such as the snowy owl and Arctic fox hunt lemmings and mice. Herds of caribou and musk oxen graze. The fur of the white Arctic hare turns brown to help the hare hide from wolves.

The Swarm

Insects are the most common Arctic animals. Harmless butterflies and bumblebees make a home on the tundra. Pests such as blackflies, tiny midges (also called no-see-ums), and mosquitoes give the tundra a bad reputation. All know how to survive the winter cold. When the weather heats up, the swarming clouds of bugs make life miserable for humans and animals!

Caribou climb, run, and stand on ice to avoid mosquitoes.

Caribou have large hooves that help them walk on snow.

Bottom of the World

Life on the Antarctic tundra tends to cluster near water. Most of Antarctica is covered with ice fields. It is too cold and dry to support plants or animals. The rocky Antarctic **Peninsula**, though, supports lichen, moss, and algae species. Two flowering plants called pearlwort and hair grass also grow there. Large animals such as seals and several kinds of penguin live at the shore. So do petrels, albatrosses, and other seabirds.

Albatrosses have large, hooked bills, which they use to snatch food from the sea.

Krummholz is a German word that means "crooked wood."

A krummholz tree

Land of Crooked Wood

Alpine tundra is found on mountains. Small plants grow in alpine tundra ecosystems because the soil thaws and drains well. Dwarf trees twisted into fantastic shapes by the freezing winds are found at the tree line boundary. Scientists call the dwarf trees krummholz.

Alpine tundra is home to plant eaters such as sheep and mountain goats. Large, fur-bearing squirrels called marmots also live there. Grasshoppers and beetles thrive in alpine tundra, too.

17

Land of the Giants

During the last Ice Age (between 110,000 and 11,700 years ago), a number of giant animals roamed the Arctic tundra searching for food and avoiding predators. Scientists call these groups of species *megafauna*, a word that means huge (mega) animals (fauna). Almost all of the Ice Age megafauna died out by the end of the Ice Age. One of the most famous species, the mammoth, survived for thousands of years afterward.

Largest deer

The Irish elk roamed Eurasia. It stood 7 feet (2 m) tall and had antlers 12 feet (3.65 m) wide.

Tundra hunter

The dire wolf, the largest known wolf species, was 5 feet (1.5 m) long and hunted in packs.

Mega-cattle

A huge cattle species called aurochs weighed more than 2,200 pounds (1,000 kilograms). The last aurochs died off in Europe in 1627.

Prehistoric people hunted
mammoths and other
large mammals.

CHAPTER 3

Tundra Then and Now

The Arctic tundra is Earth's youngest ecosystem. It formed 10,000 years ago, after the end of the last Ice Age. Before then, tundra spread across regions farther south. There, tundra lichens, mosses, and plants fed prehistoric animals such as horses and bison. Human hunters walked vast distances hunting **prey** such as reindeer and mammoth. These prehistoric people wore fur clothing and stored meat in cellars dug out of the near-frozen soil above the permafrost.

Early hunters sometimes used spears to hunt mammoths.

A New World

Between 40,000 and 14,000 years ago, the Ice Age glaciers formed out of frozen snow. Because the glaciers did not melt, there was less water in the ocean. This exposed the ocean floor. The floor of today's **Bering Strait** became dry land. The land formed a bridge that connected Eurasia with what is today Alaska. Scientists believe the land bridge was an ecosystem of cold, dry, flat grasslands. Humans crossed the land bridge, probably while hunting, and entered North America.

The Bering Strait separates Alaska from Russia.

The Bering Strait is about 53 miles (85 km) wide.

Early Native Americans made clothing from the skins of animals.

The Long Walk

North America's ice sheets probably kept the hunters from moving beyond today's Alaska and Yukon Territory at first. As the Ice Age ended, the ice sheets broke up. The hunters and their families wandered out of the Arctic to explore. They settled in North and South America. Scientists believe the **descendants** of these explorers became the many Native American peoples.

Above the Arctic Circle

Humans probably started crossing the Bering land bridge during the summer months. That is when the tundra warms up and there is more daylight. Because of the way Earth tilts as it rotates around the sun, the northern latitudes get a lot of sunlight during the summer. The Arctic Circle is the southern border of the Arctic region. There, the sun stays up around the clock on the first day of summer. Farther north, the sun remains in the sky for days, weeks, or even months.

In the Arctic, the sun stays above the horizon all night long for part of the summer.

Longyearbyen, Norway, is the world's most northern town.

Land of the Midnight Sun

The Arctic Circle crosses Alaska and Canada's three northern territories. It also crosses Greenland, Iceland, Norway, Sweden, Finland, and Russia. Each of these places can claim to be the Land of the Midnight Sun. The Norwegian island chain of Svalbard is the northernmost place in Europe where people live. There, the sun rises on April 19 and sets on August 23. One summer "day" at the North Pole lasts six months!

Children playing under the midnight sun in Canada.

Too Much Sunshine

The midnight sun affects human beings in unusual ways. One common problem is that they have trouble sleeping. Other people feel hyper, or too energetic. Over time, they may feel irritable or find it hard to concentrate. Visitors and newcomers tend to experience the problems more than people who are used to the long days. In some places, people have fun with the midnight sun. Icelanders, for example, hold an all-night golf tournament.

Arctic Workers

Few people live in the tundra. Those who have settled there in the past tended to be hunters or herders. Today, the Sami people of northern Scandinavia and Finland still keep herds of reindeer. The animals run free most of the time. In the summer, however, the Sami go on a roundup using helicopters. The Sami sell reindeer meat and use the animals' skins to make warm blankets.

A Sami man feeds reindeer.

Reindeer are called caribou in North America.

27

Rich in Natural Resources

In the last hundred years, resources such as gold and petroleum (oil) have brought thousands of people to Arctic regions. Workers at Alaska's Prudhoe Bay send oil south through the Trans-Alaska Pipeline. Arctic workers face challenges. For example, food is expensive because almost everything must be flown in or shipped in. A gallon of milk in Barrow, Alaska, costs about eight dollars.

The TransAlaska Pipeline is 800 miles (1,300 km) long.

Frozen Flu

A deadly flu virus swept the world in 1918. In the mid-1990s, scientists came up with a plan to find it again to study it. A San Francisco scientist believed the disease survived in the bodies of people buried in permafrost in 1918. A retired doctor named Johan Hultin volunteered to go to Alaska to exhume, or dig up, the body of a flu victim. The plan worked. Hultin found tissue samples that contained the 1918 flu.

Graves of flu victims

The 1918 virus was called the Spanish flu.

29

Climate change is warming the habitat of polar bears, making it harder for them to find food.

CHAPTER 4

Species in Danger

The tundra is a fragile ecosystem. Changes in temperature or sunlight can cause a tundra region to expand (if the climate turns colder) or to shrink (if the climate turns warmer). Climate change also affects habitats, the places where animals live. If the change is extreme, some species may find it hard to survive. They may become **extinct** like mammoths and dire wolves.

 Polar bears have rough paw pads that keep them from slipping on ice.

Plants with deep roots cannot live in the tundra.

Valuable Species

Tundra ecosystems have less **biodiversity** than warmer ones. They contain a smaller number of plant and animal species. Changes often have a greater effect on a low-biodiversity ecosystem than on an ecosystem with more living things. If an animal species dies out on the tundra, there may be no other species to take its place. Ecosystems with more living things have more possible replacements.

The extinction of a species stresses the other living things that depend on it. This is especially true in the tundra. For example, wolves on Arctic islands in Canada feed on Peary caribou. Warming temperatures have helped reduce the number of Peary caribou. There are few other prey for animals to eat in the tundra ecosystem. If the Peary caribou becomes extinct, the wolves will have a hard time finding a meal.

The Peary caribou was named after explorer Robert Peary.

CHAPTER 5

Why the Tundra Matters

One of the changes taking place on the tundra may affect climates around the world. Permafrost locks in harmful greenhouse gases. Warmer temperatures in the Arctic cause permafrost to thaw. Greenhouse gases are then released into the air. When too much greenhouse gas is added to the atmosphere, problems are created.

Humans add billions of tons of harmful gases to the atmosphere every year. →

The Carbon Dioxide Problem

Carbon dioxide (dye-OX-ide) is one greenhouse gas in the atmosphere. It traps the heat that is escaping Earth. The result is warmer temperatures and climate change. This is known as the greenhouse effect.

Thawing permafrost accounts for only a small part of the rising greenhouse gas levels. The burning of fossil fuels such as coal and petroleum has caused about 75 percent of the increase in recent decades.

Factories release large amounts of greenhouse gases.

Methane Menace

Carbon dioxide is not the only threat created by thawing permafrost. Methane is another greenhouse gas locked in tundra soil. Ice crystals trap the methane. When warm temperatures cause the crystals to melt, methane escapes into the atmosphere. Then it adds to the greenhouse effect just as carbon dioxide does. But there is one difference. Methane's effect on the warming of the atmosphere is 20 times stronger than that of carbon dioxide!

Timeline of the Tundra

16,000 B.C.E.

The Bering Strait land bridge forms during the Ice Age.

10,000 B.C.E.

The Ice Age ends.

The Big Melt

A rise in worldwide temperatures would change the climate of many places. It would also thaw more permafrost. Then, even more methane and carbon dioxide would be released. Warmer seawater could allow even more of the gases to escape from the bottom of the Arctic Ocean, where there is permafrost below the seafloor. As warmer temperatures melt Arctic glaciers, sea levels will rise. That will affect Earth's climate, too.

1,700 B.C.E.

All mammoths are extinct due to the climate change following the end of the Ice Age.

8,000 B.C.E.

Much land that was once tundra has warmed and become other types of ecosystems.

Runaway Methane

When methane gas is added to the atmosphere, the change is permanent. Its effect on the environment cannot be stopped once it has been released. Scientists worry that a lot of methane gas in the atmosphere could change weather patterns in just a short period of time.

Some experts believe that rather than a methane release, an asteroid crash caused the Permian period to end. ➡

Some experts think that a huge methane release occurred about 251 million years ago. That was the end of the Permian period, when most of Earth's animals became extinct. Between 90 and 95 percent of all sea species died out. Seventy percent of those on land vanished. It is possible that methane release may have played a part in causing so many animals to become extinct. No one will ever know for sure.

Dimetrodons and most other species on Earth went extinct at the end of the Permian period.

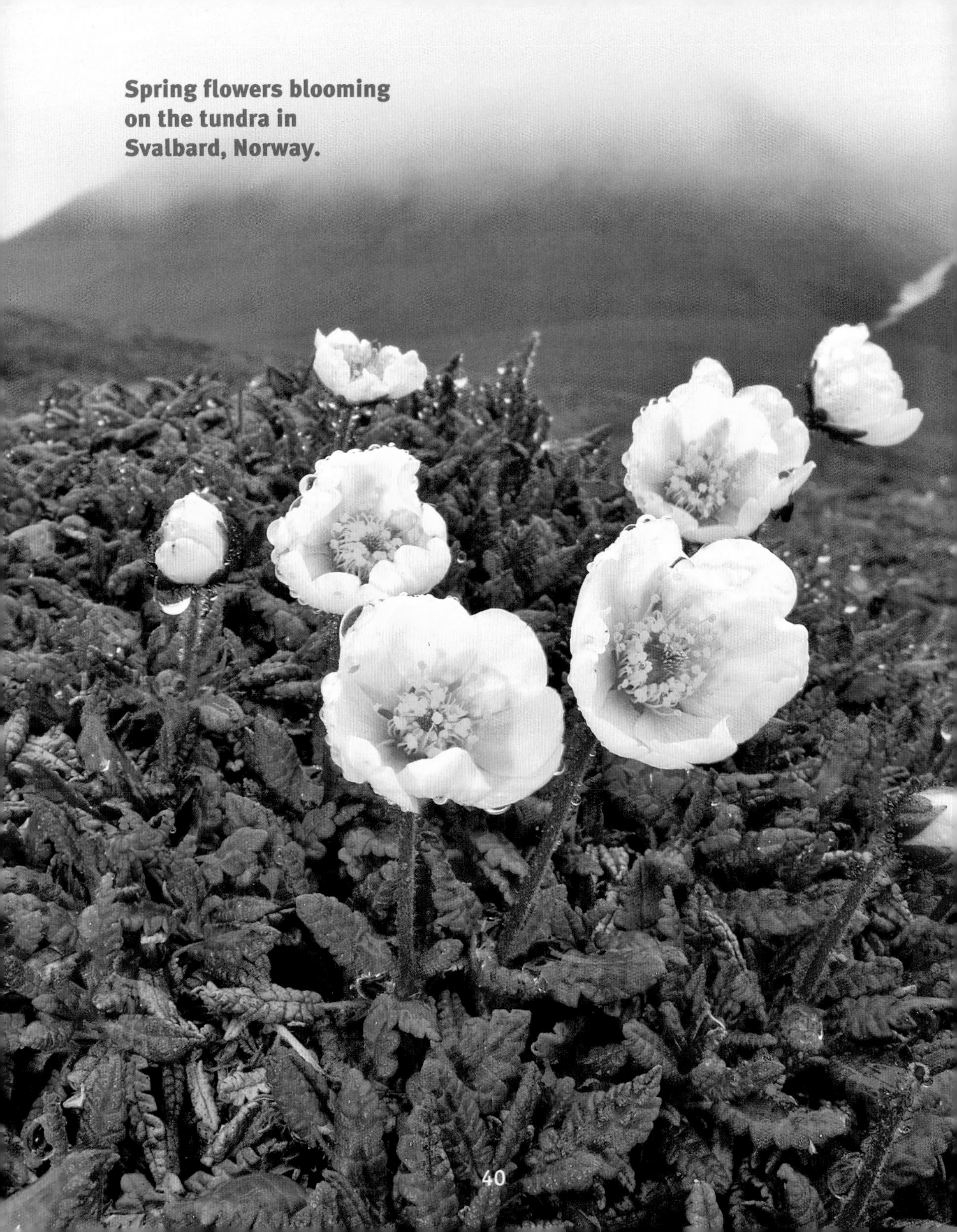

Spring flowers blooming on the tundra in Svalbard, Norway.

CHAPTER 6

The Tundra and Our Future

It is already clear that warmer temperatures are affecting the permafrost. In many places, the active layer reaches deeper than it did before. The permanently frozen layer beneath that starts deeper as a result. Scientists continue to study what happens as the permafrost thaws. They want to learn more about methane release and other possible reasons for global warming.

As more permafrost thaws, different species will grow in the tundra.

The tundra is a rugged, frozen ecosystem. Protecting it is important if we want to save the animals and plants that live there. Scientists also think it is important to understand the role that thawing permafrost plays in climate change. They have known for a long time that the Arctic holds rich deposits of fossil fuels and precious metals. As time goes on, we may find that the tundra contains even more valuable resources. Such discoveries could be the key to our future. ★

Many people who visit the tundra come to appreciate its delicate beauty.

Amount of land that is tundra: 14.3 percent

Age of current tundra: About 10,000 years old

Height of large pingo: 300 ft. (90 m)

Typical rainfall on tundra in a year: Less than 10 in. (25 cm)

Number of tundra plant species: 1,700

Width of the Bering Strait: 53 mi. (85 km)

Length of summer "day" at North Pole: 6 months

Width of an Irish elk's antlers: 12 ft. (3.65 m)

Latitude of the Arctic Circle: 66.5° north

Did you find the truth?

(F) Tundra is too cold for insects.

(T) Permafrost contains methane.

Resources

Books

Clarke, Penny. *Life in the Tundra*. New York: Children's Press, 2005.

Dayton, Connor. *Tundra Animals*. New York: PowerKids Press, 2009.

Green, Jen. *Life on the Tundra*. New York: Gareth Stevens Publishing, 2010.

Johansson, Philip. *The Frozen Tundra: A Web of Life*. Berkeley Heights, NJ: Enslow Publishers, 2004.

Levy, Janey. *Discovering the Arctic Tundra*. New York: PowerKids Press, 2008.

Roza, Greg. *Tundra: Life in a Frozen Landscape*. New York: Rosen Publishing Group, 2009.

Tagliaferro, Linda. *Explore the Tundra*. Mankato, MN: Capstone Press, 2007.

Tocci, Salvatore. *Arctic Tundra: Life at the North Pole*. New York: Franklin Watts, 2005.

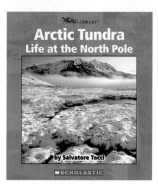

Organizations and Web Sites

Animal Planet: Map of World Biomes

http://animal.discovery.com/guides/mammals/habitat/map.html
Check out an interactive map, and learn more about tundra mammals.

National Geographic Explorer!: Featured Quick Flick

http://magma.nationalgeographic.com/ngexplorer/0211/quickflicks/
Explore the tundra as you watch a short clip.

National Geographic: Tundra

http://environment.nationalgeographic.com/environment/habitats/tundra-profile/
Read about the tundra and the threats it faces.

Places to Visit

Point Defiance Zoo & Aquarium: Arctic Tundra

5400 N. Pearl St.
Tacoma, WA 98407
(253) 591-5337
www.pdza.org
This Arctic tundra exhibit houses reindeer, Arctic foxes, and more.

Toronto Zoo: Tundra Trek

361A Old Finch Avenue
Toronto, Ontario, Canada
M1B 5K7
(416) 392-5929
www.torontozoo.com
Don't miss the state-of-the-art polar bear habitat at this exhibit.

Important Words

active layer (AK-tiv LAY-ur)—the top, melting layer of permafrost

Bering Strait (BEHR-ing STRATE)—the waterway separating Eurasia and Alaska

biodiversity (BY-oh-duh-VER-suh-tee)—the number of different life-forms in an ecosystem

descendants (dee-SEN-dents)—people born from an older ancestor; a child is a descendant of a parent

ecosystem (EE-koh-sis-tuhm)—a community of plants and animals and the environment they live in

extinct (ek-STINGKT)—no longer in existence

latitudes (LAT-uh-toodz)—a measurement of how far a place is from the equator

peninsula (puh-NIN-suh-luh)—a piece of land with water on all sides but one

permafrost (PUR-muh-frawst) frozen soil beneath the surface of tundra

predators (PREH-duh-turz)—animals that live by eating other animals

prey (PRAY)—an animal used as food by a predator

sedges (SEJ-iz) grasslike plants with solid stems and small flowers

stunt (STUNT)—to stop normal growth

Index

Page numbers in **bold** indicate illustrations

About the Author

Peter Benoit is educated as a mathematician but has many other interests. He has taught and tutored high school and college students for many years, mostly in math and science. He also runs summer workshops for writers and students of literature. Mr. Benoit has also written more than 2,000 poems. His life has been one committed to learning. He lives in Greenwich, New York.